Solo Violin

4

Solo Violin

Violin Concerto

I

PHILIP GLASS
(1987)

Philip Glass

Violin Concerto

(1987)

Violin

Chester Music

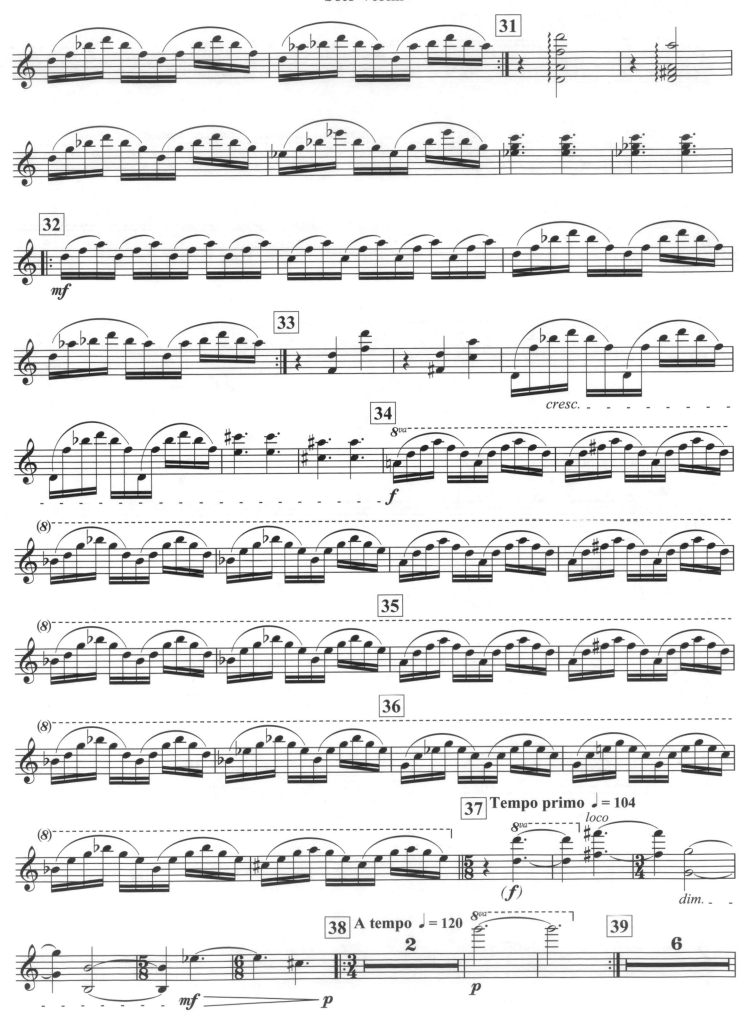

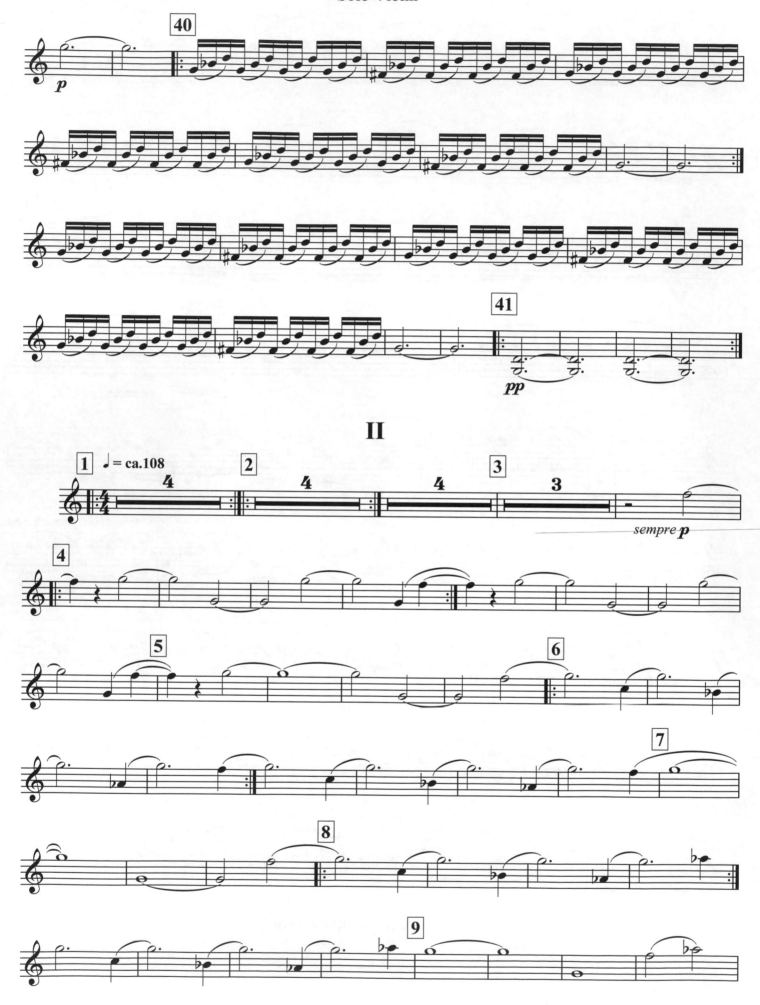

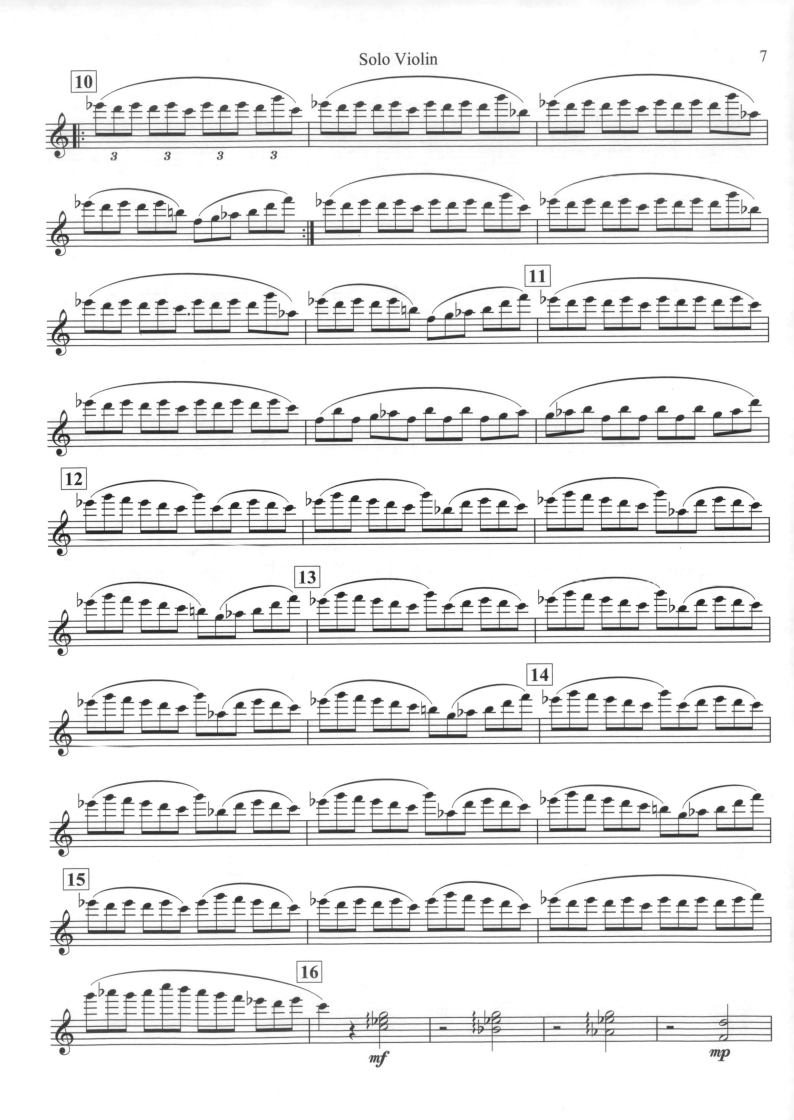

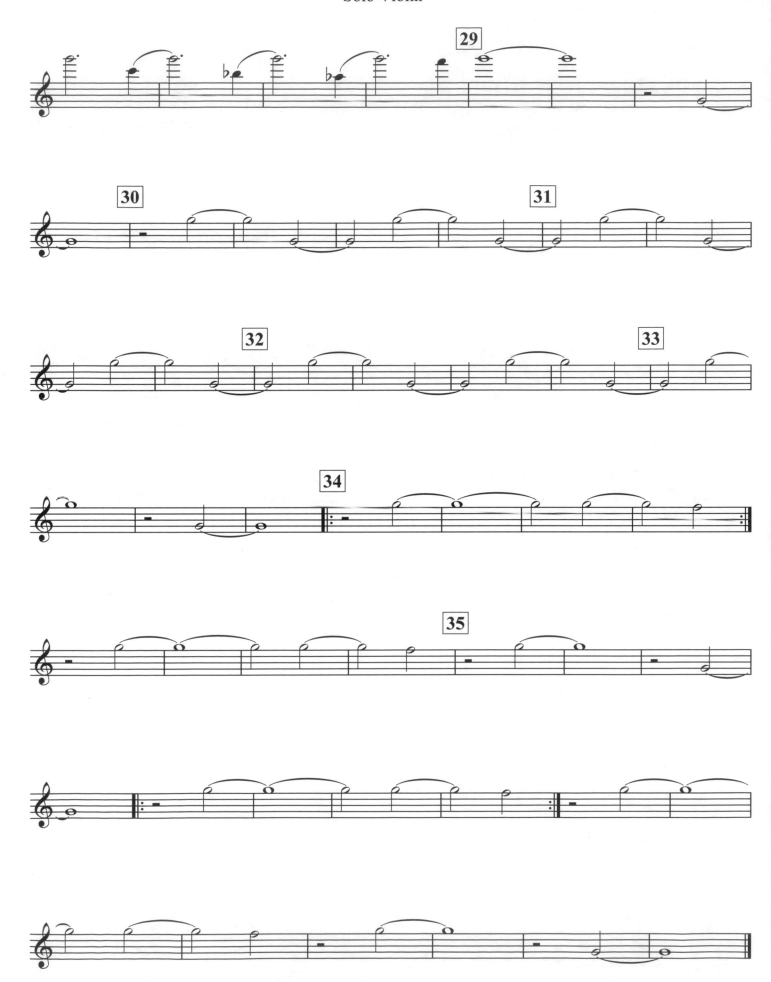

III

Selected concert works for violin

CONCERTOS

Richard Rodney Bennett
Violin Concerto
Solo part with piano *NOV360090*

Witold Lutoslawski
Chain 2
score *CH55874*
violin part only *CH60932*

Peter Maxwell Davies
Concerto for Violin
Solo part with piano *CH55915*

John McCabe
Concerto for Violin (Sinfonia Concertante)
Solo part with piano *NOV120306*

Michael Nyman
Concerto for Violin and Orchestra
Solo part with piano *CH70235*

Kaija Saariaho
Graal Théâtre
Score on hire
violin part only *SOS05210*

Hugh Wood
Violin Concerto
Solo part with piano *CT55152*

VIOLIN AND PIANO

Richard Rodney Bennett
Six Country Dances *NOV950600*

Brian Elias
Fantasia *SOS00329*

Nicola LeFanu
Abstracts and a Frame *NOV120461*

Witold Lutoslawski
Partita *CH55795*
Subito *CH61039*

John McCabe
Star Preludes *NOV120535*

Michael Nyman
Miserere Paraphrase *CH61097*
On the Fiddle *CH61332*

Giles Swayne
Duo *NOV120502*

John Tavener
Fragment for the Virgin *CH69465-01*

Judith Weir
Music for 247 Strings *NOV120573*

Hugh Wood
Poem *CH61140*

The Violin: A Collection
works by Armstrong, Arnold, Bennett, Chapple, Falla, Glass, Lutoslawski, Maxwell Davies, Nyman, Poulenc, Saariaho, Talbot, Tavener and Weir
Solo part with piano *CH69641*

www.chesternovello.com

CHESTER MUSIC
part of The Music Sales Group
8/9 Frith Street, LONDON, W1D 3JB
Exclusive Distributors: Music Sales Ltd
Newmarket Road, Bury St. Edmunds, Suffolk, IP33 3YB

Order No. DU10368

Philip Glass

Violin Concerto

(1987)

Piano reduction by Charles Abramovich

Philip Glass's *Violin Concerto* was commissioned by the American Composers'
Orchestra, who gave the first performance, conducted by Dennis Russell
Davies, on 5 April 1987 at Carnegie Hall, New York City. It is dedicated to
Dennis Russell Davies and Paul Zukofsky, soloist at the premiere.

Chester Music
(part of The Music Sales Group)
8/9, Frith Street, London W1D 3JB, England
Tel +44 (0)20 7434 0066; Fax +44 (0)20 7287 6329

Sales and hire:
Music Sales Distribution Centre,
Newmarket Road,
Bury St. Edmunds,
Suffolk IP33 3YB, England
Tel +44 (0)1284 702600; Fax +44 (0)1284 768301

www.chesternovello.com email: music@musicsales.co.uk

Violin Concerto

PHILIP GLASS
(1987)

I

3

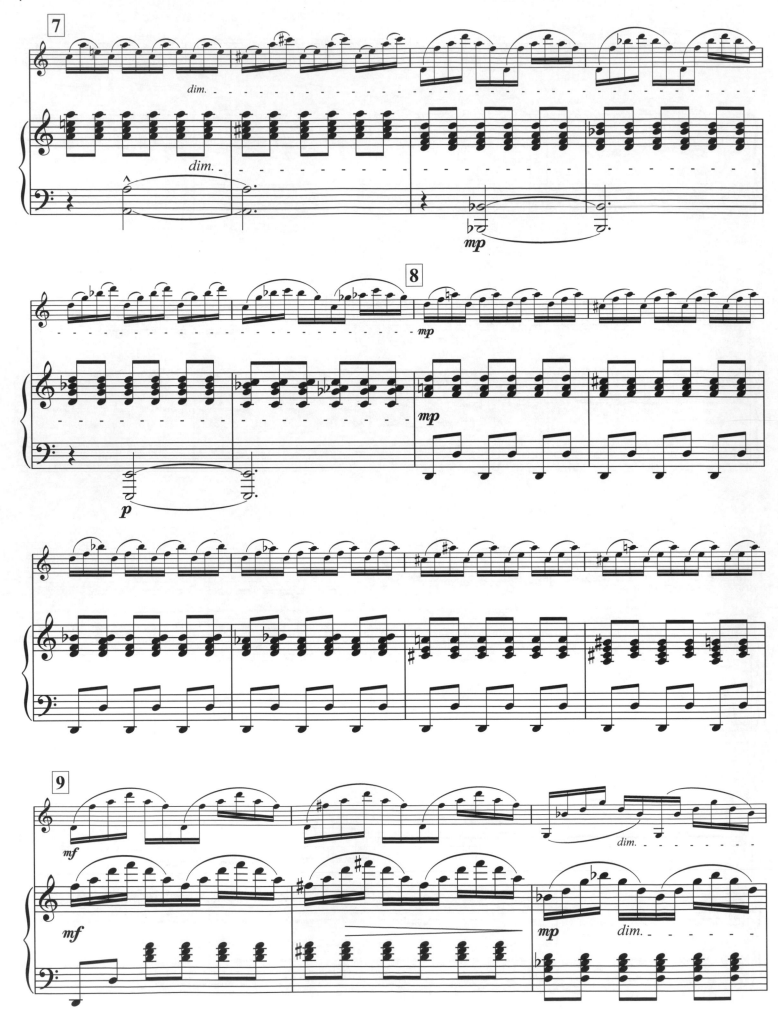

6

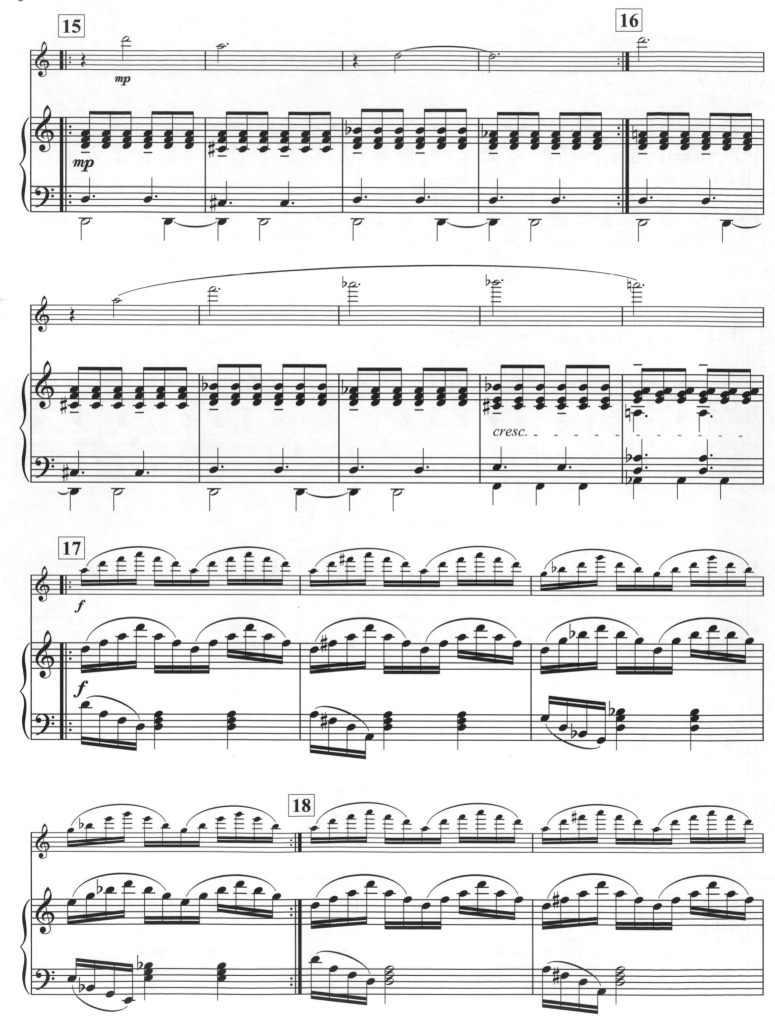

18

19

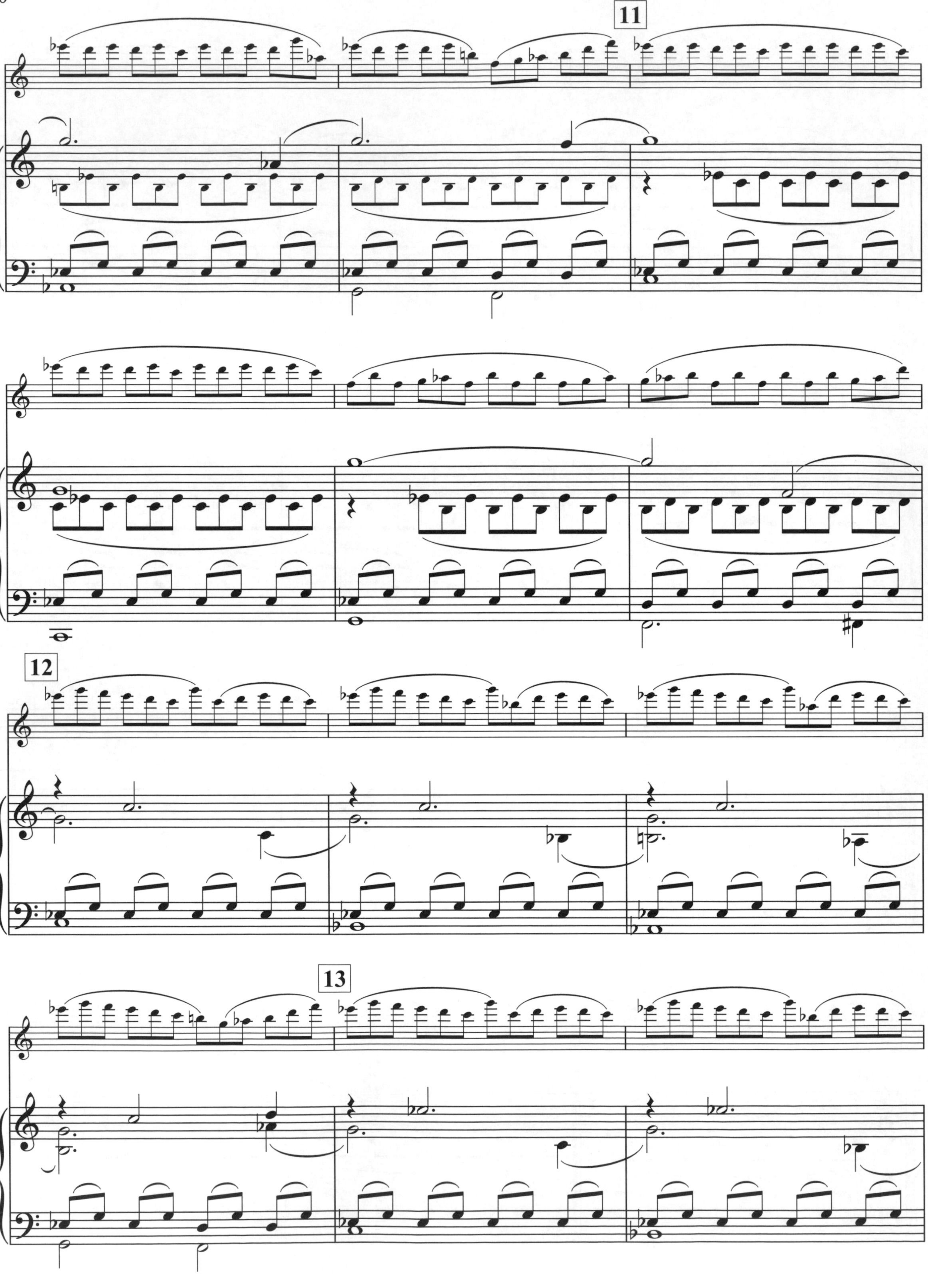
11
12
13

24

28

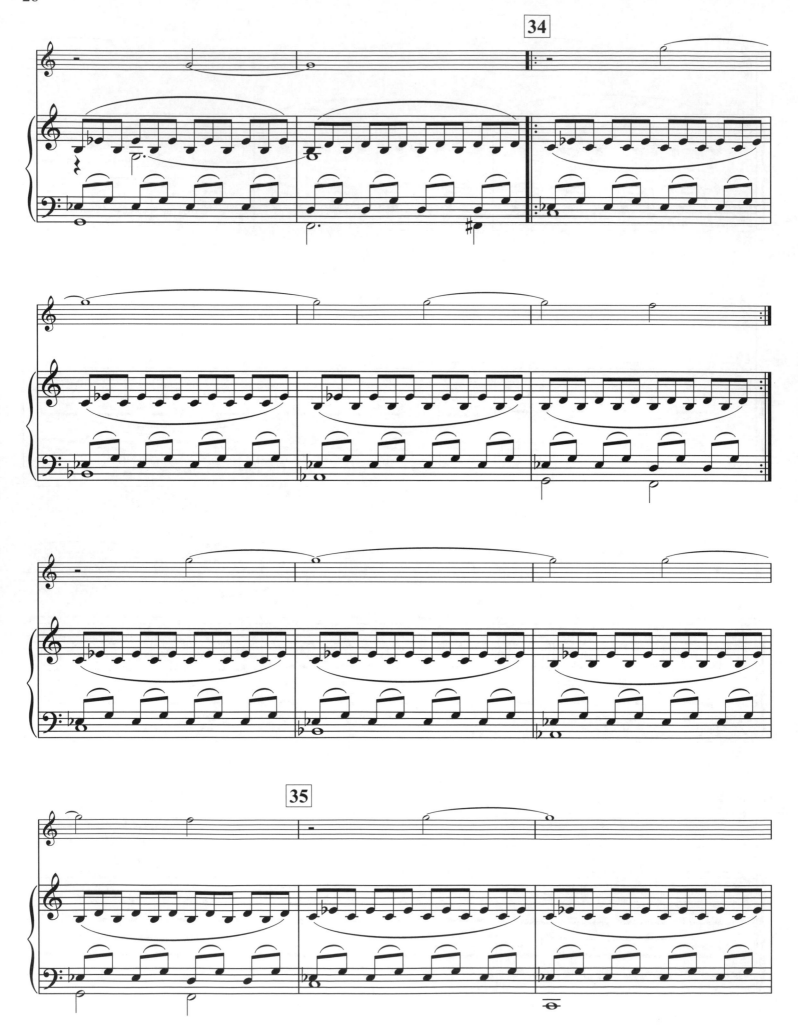

III

34

41

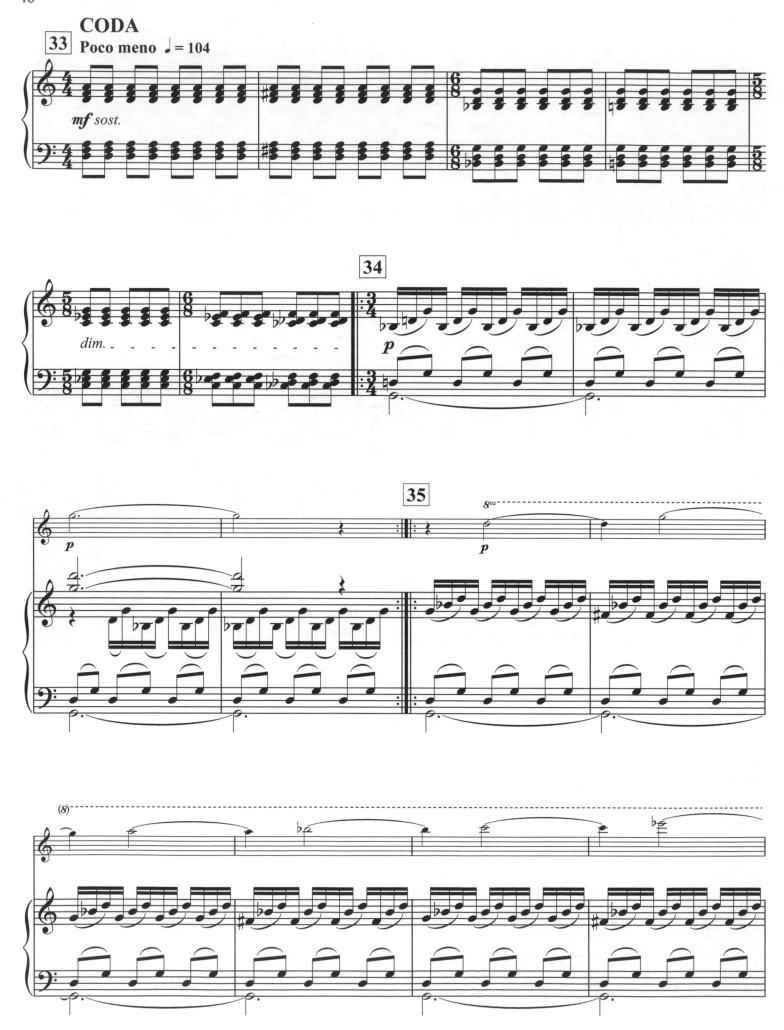

48

11/06(60414)